THE CASE FOR CHRISTIAN PREPAREDNESS

FAITH AND PREPPING FOR SURVIVAL

FORREST GARVIN

Dedicated to my family, Teresa, Caleb, Cody and Cassidy

CONTENTS

Acknowledgments   i

1   The Case for Christian Preparedness   3

2   Why Christians Should Prepare   10

3   What Does the Bible Say About Prepping?   18

4   Stockpiling, the Beginning of All Prepping   27

5   Practical Skills to Help You Survive   32

6   Faith, Our Most Important Prep   46

7   One Last Thing You Need   55

    About The Author & Resources   63

ACKNOWLEDGMENTS

I would like to give a shout out to:
Travis Currin, Mark D. Gott, Ryan Mitchell,
Eric Parlow, and David Miller for their help
and constant encouragement

Chapter 1.

The Case for Christian Preparedness

The modern prepping movement, now in its fifth year, is primarily a conservative movement. It is driven by the combination of pressing concerns about our government, political unrest around the world, natural disasters, and a myriad of other tensions. When Donald Trump was elected president in 2016, some of the political concerns lessened, but many people believe his leadership is only a delay of the impending financial and moral decay of America.

We, the American people, are in as much danger today as we have ever been. Yes, the president met with Kim Jung-un of North Korea and there are peace talks going on, but that has happened before. North Korea's strategy is to build up its military capabilities, threaten other countries, and force them into peace talks. Their objective is to wring concessions out of these countries. In spite of the meeting with president Trump, North Korea is still building nuclear arms and missiles, even though they aren't doing any new testing right now. In fact, in true form, they refuse to stop until South Korea, America and our other allies cave into their list of demands.

North Korea is not the only threat on the horizon. Iran is still actively seeking to join the ranks of nations with nuclear arms and have been working towards that goal for decades. They, like North Korea, have publicly declared their intent to use such weapons against the United States.

Should Americans be concerned about these blatant threats? Can these foes really destroy great America? The most effective way for these rogue nations or terrorist groups to use nuclear arms against the United States would be through a high-altitude EMP (electromagnetic pulse). Such an attack, if properly planned and executed, would destroy the country's electrical grids, plunge the nation into darkness, and destroy all our electrically operated devices. Recovery would be slow if at all.

Estimates by the US Department of Defense's EMP Commission Report say up to 90 percent of our population would die within the first year, mostly from starvation. If we ever did recover and restore the electrical grid, it would likely take decades. Of course, this is one area of serious concern. However, it is by no means the biggest one out there.

Statistically speaking, we are much more likely to suffer devastation caused by a natural disaster than we are from a nuclear weapon landing on our city or an EMP taking out the grid. We've all seen the havoc and damage that hurricanes can cause – loss of life and property, storm surges and so forth. Furthermore, hurricanes are not the only natural disasters Mother Nature has to offer. Earthquakes, tornados, tsunamis, and droughts are all disasters every state in our country is subject to.

WHAT IS PREPPING?

The whole idea of prepping is to be ready for disasters when and if they happen regardless of the type, size, intensity or duration. Since there is no way for us to stop them, and we rarely know their timing or the extent of devastation they will cause, it only makes sense to be ready when they do come. That means having the necessary knowledge, skills, equipment, and supplies to survive without our massive infrastructure to support us.

Throughout human history, our ancestors have always prepared for disasters. For most, winter was a major disaster. The cold temperatures and snow made farming impossible, so the people had to depend on whatever food they could grow and preserve in the warmer months. Only in some of the warmer climates near the equator could people step out of their doors year round and pick food off the trees.

Prepping can also go far beyond preparing for natural disasters. When the Ebola outbreak of 2014 was ravaging West Africa, there was concern that it might spread beyond that area via air travel, infecting the rest of the world. Many in the prepping community made provision for that, stockpiling hazmat suits and learning how to protect their families from the disease, should it come to their communities.

Then there are some disasters, which are so extreme, they change our lives in a permanent way. Preppers call these events TEOTWAWKI (the end of the world as we know it) events. That is not to say they believe such events are the true "end of the world," but rather, that they will be severe enough to radically change the way of life for many people. Instead of returning to normal, they will end up finding a new normal.

For many people living in the New Orleans area, Hurricane Katrina was a TEOTWAWKI event. They didn't even bother to go back home because their homes were destroyed, and their possessions were lost. They took whatever money their insurance paid them, whatever government aid they could get, and moved on elsewhere to start their lives anew.

Modern society is highly dependent on the massive

infrastructure we have built. We find it very difficult to survive without the goods and services provided – electric power, food in the grocery store. Few are truly able to sustain themselves on their own. Should a TEOTWAWKI event or even a lesser event occur, the average American has no idea what to do. A TEOTWAWKI event will prevent the country's infrastructure from functioning and meeting our needs. Most people would have no idea where to find water and how to purify it, how to heat their homes without the furnace running or where they could find food. The majority of people can't even start a fire without lighter fluid or gasoline to help them.

Preppers, especially the very experienced ones, learn self-sufficiency. They accept as fact that the infrastructure we all depend on will fail someday whether only for a short time or permanently. In preparation for such a happening, they may try to turn their homes into urban homesteads, growing their own food, as well as having some means of harvesting water and producing their own electrical power.

It's More Than Just Stockpiling Food

Most people begin prepping by stockpiling food, perhaps something as simple as rice and beans. But before long, they will often move beyond that seeking to find ways of meeting life's other needs. The idea is to have some means of providing for all of the body's basic survival needs. These include:

1. Maintaining body heat
2. Purified water
3. Food
4. Fire
5. First-aid
6. Self-defense

Many express the top needs in what is referred to as the "rule of 3s," which states that the human body can only live for 30 minutes without maintaining core body heat, 3 days without water, and 30 days without food. While those numbers may not be exactly correct, the relationship between them is right and gives us a good idea of our true priorities.

It can take a great deal of specialized equipment and lots of supplies to meet the six basic needs mentioned earlier. However, preppers need to stockpile an even greater survival tool – knowledge, specifically, the knowledge of how to do a myriad of things that we, as a society have forgotten how to do. We have totally depended on the infrastructure or electrical power to do them for us.

EMP is often used as a worst-case disaster scenario for preparedness planning. In the event that an EMP or other attack destroys our power grid, many say we would be thrown back to living as our ancestors did in the 1800s. But it would be worse than that. It would be a regression to a lifestyle completely unknown to us. Our ancestors understood how to live without electrical power and had the tools they needed to do so, but most of us don't have that today.

Learning the necessary skills to survive without power, whether in the wilderness or in our homes, is an important part of prepping. Should a cataclysmic event ever happen in the United States, the ones with the best chances of survival are those who have the knowledge.

Chapter 2.

Why Christians Should Prepare

Some people say Christians shouldn't prepare for such occurrences. Instead, they should simply depend on God to take care of them. Personally, I am a firm believer in God's power and providence to take care of my family. Nevertheless, trusting in God and being prepared are not mutually exclusive. Good reason and Scripture testify to this. Hence, at the same time, I am a firm believer in being prepared. This doesn't mean that I don't have faith. Rather, I join my faith with my preparedness in taking care of my family's needs.

When Israel was wandering in the wilderness, God provided them with manna and quail to eat. But He only made that provision six days a week. Therefore, each and every week, the people suffered a natural disaster in that there was no food laying on the ground for them to gather on the Sabbath. If they did not gather enough food for two days on the sixth day of the week, they went hungry on the seventh.

Did the Israelites lack faith because they gathered twice as much manna on the sixth day? By no means. In fact, they were obedient to God's command to do so.

Behold, I will rain bread from heaven for you. And the people shall go out and gather a certain quota every day, that I may test them, whether they will walk in My law or not. 5 And it shall be in the sixth day that they shall prepare what they bring in, and it shall be twice as much as they gather daily (Exodus 16:4-5).

Here, we see God's provision for His people through the giving of the bread or manna. But at the same time, God also commands them to prepare for a time of lack, a time when He made it clear He would not be providing. Even more telling than this was the fact He did that as a test to see if they would obey His Law. Had they not prepared and simply depended on Him to provide, they would have been disobedient!

Of course, some people disobeyed by gathering too much; they were trying to save beyond the sixth day. However, the extra they gathered "bred worms and stank" (Exodus 16:20). Others disobeyed in another way, for "Some of the people went out on the seventh day to gather, but they found none" (Exodus 16:27).

The Bible records in the book of Genesis, another time when God directed people to prepare through Joseph, one of Jacob's 12 sons (one of the 12 patriarchs). In this case, God did not speak through a prophet as He had done through Moses. Rather, He used Joseph to interpret a dream He gave to Pharaoh, the king of Egypt

(Genesis 41:1-7).

None of Pharaoh's magicians could interpret his dreams, but his butler remembered Joseph, who in prison, had interpreted a dream of his (Genesis 41:11-13). So Joseph was brought forth out of the prison, and he interpreted Pharaoh's dream for him (Genesis 41:15-32). Can we say God wasn't in this? Joseph didn't. He gave God the glory for it.

> *It is not in me; God will give Pharaoh an*
> *answer of peace (Genesis 41:16).*

It is clear that God is the one who gave that dream to Pharaoh, even though Scripture doesn't say so. It is even clearer that He gave the interpretation to Joseph. Obviously, God orchestrated the entire event. He not only arranged for Joseph to be promoted as the prime minister of Egypt, but He made provision for Jacob (Israel) and his 11 other sons, along with their families, to be cared for in the midst of a drought. Had God not done that, the lineage of Abraham would have died out.

As the prime minister of Egypt, Joseph created a national prepping system, storing up grain for the coming drought, which God had revealed through Joseph's interpretation of Pharaoh's dream. Evidently, Joseph was not only a man of faith but also a prepper who obeyed God by preparing for a coming disaster.

If faith and prepping could come together in Joseph's life, why can't they come together in ours as well?

Scripture clearly shows that God expects us to operate in faith. However, it is also easy to see that He expects us to work and do what is necessary to take care of ourselves. In a way, we can say that the latter became necessary. It is part of the curse of the fall recorded in Genesis Chapter 3 where God told Adam: "Cursed is the ground for your sake; in toil you shall eat of it all the days of your life" (Genesis 3:17b). That is pretty clear.

We see that work, and by extension, prepping, is a biblical principle. God created this world in such a way that we don't just work to eat today, but rather, like the ant, we work for what we will need to eat tomorrow. In others words, we must work to survive.

> *Go to the ant, you sluggard! Consider her ways and be wise, which, having no captain, overseer or ruler, provides her supplies in the summer, and gathers her food in the harvest. How long will you slumber, o sluggard? When will you rise from your sleep? A little sleep, a little slumber, a little folding of the hands to sleep – so shall your poverty come on you like a prowler, and your need like an armed man (Proverbs 6:6-11).*

If there was ever a part of God's creation that typifies disaster preparedness, it is that hardworking ant. No wonder King Solomon used the ant as an example of good work ethics. And what was his admonition? If you aren't like the ant, working hard and storing up for tomorrow, poverty will overtake you. Yes, it will, and that's exactly what will happen to those who are not prepared for a disaster.

If the book of Proverbs has any message for us, it is this: God desires us to live each and every day operating in wisdom – not just any wisdom either, but His wisdom. God's wisdom and the world's wisdom are not one and the same, and of the two, His is far superior. Hence, we should live by it.

God's wisdom teaches us to look at the world around us and see what is happening, not for mere knowledge but for survival. While we may not know of every disaster before it befalls us, we can see the signs of disaster all around and that they are happening all the time. Our national debt is unsustainable. Violence is prevalent in the world, especially the barbarity fomented by terrorist groups, which is increasing. Ample evidence exists all around to show us we need to prepare.

> *A prudent man foresees evil and hides himself;*
> *the simple pass on and are punished (Proverbs*
> *27:12).*

So the question for us is which type of people will we be? Do we rightly count ourselves amongst the prudent who foresee evil and create a place to hide from it? Or are we nothing more than the simple who are punished? The book of Proverbs doesn't say many good things about those simple people. Actually, the writer makes it very clear we should not be a part of them. No, we should be the wise and prudent who do what is necessary to take care of ourselves and our families as we serve God all the days of our lives.

COMING DISASTERS FORETOLD

Most Christians have heard that we are living in the end-times. Time after time, one preacher or another has come up with a date thinking they had unraveled the mystery of the ages and knew when the rapture was going to occur. While all of those dates have been proven to be false, one thing is clear: we are living in the end-times.

Some of the best-known verses about the end-times mention disasters. Jesus said,

> *But when you hear of wars and rumors of wars, do not be troubled; for such things must happen, but the end is not yet. 8 For nation will rise against nation, and kingdom against kingdom. And there will be earthquakes in various places, and there will be famines and troubles. These are the beginning of sorrows (Mark 13:7-8).*

Wars, earthquakes, famines, and troubles — and that's before the Great Tribulation even begins. God has informed us of His plans, and they don't look pretty. In fact, they look downright dangerous. From that one verse alone, we can see that the closer to the end we get, the more we are headed to dangerous times.

It doesn't matter what sort of end-time theology you hold because we're not talking about preparing for the Armageddon. Rather, we're talking about a time that Jesus referred to in those verses as "the beginning of sorrows." But what is this beginning of sorrows? It is the time before any of the events mentioned in the book of Revelation. A time in which the world is getting ready for what is to come.

We must remember that what we refer to as "supernatural" isn't something spooky, mystic or some spiritual force. The supernatural are things God uses in not so natural ways. The ravens that brought Elijah food in the morning and in the evening (1 Kings 17:6) were real, natural ravens. God directed them to do something that was outside their nature. That was a supernatural work.

Some geologists have tried to dispute the account of Joshua and the people of Israel crossing the Jordan River (Joshua 3:14-16) by saying there was an earthquake upstream, which caused the course of the river to change. Because of it, the river stopped flowing for some hours. OK, let's assume they are right. If so, who caused the earthquake to happen at just the right time? Who made the river run dry at the very time the priests carrying the ark stepped into the overflowing waters of the Jordan River? God did! He made that a supernatural event.

I mention this because the supernatural events of the Tribulation as explained in the book of Revelation, will all be natural events, for which scientists will likely come up with natural explanations. However, we have already been shown that those events will be directed by God. That's what will make them supernatural. Likewise, the disasters that occur during the time known as the beginning of sorrows: wars, earthquakes, famines, and troubles will all be directed by God. It will be a time in which the earth groans in preparation for the birth of something new.

According to recent studies, the number of natural and geophysical disasters taking place each year is noticeably skyrocketing. Scientists state that the surge in climatic disasters is due to both man-made and natural elements. However, contrary to the popular belief, this increase is not attributed to global warming.

We won't escape this time (unless we die beforehand), regardless of what we believe about the end- times. The beginning of sorrows happens before the 70th week of Daniel timeline begins. We will be forced to live through those wars, earthquakes, famines, and troubles. The question is how well will we manage to live through them, especially if there is no natural infrastructure to help us?

Chapter 3.

What Does the Bible Say About Prepping?

You won't find the word "prepping" in the Bible no matter how hard you try or what translation you use. It's just not there. That's probably because the modern prepping movement is something new in the world, conceived a couple of thousand years after the New Testament was written. But does that mean prepping isn't something Scripture supports? By no means. While the Bible doesn't mention the idea of prepping by name, it does talk about seed-time and harvest. Once we understand that the whole planting cycle is predicated upon surviving the next winter, it is clear that God not only endorses prepping, but He built it into the very nature of a fallen world.

Granted, wintertime wasn't a major concern for the Israelites, since the nation of Israel lies at about 31° north longitude. To put that in perspective, it's at the same longitude as the Gulf Coast of Mississippi, Alabama, Louisiana, and the Florida panhandle. In other words, the cold wasn't enough of an issue to keep the Israelites of Old Testament times from planting in what most of us call winter. Yet, we know from the historical record, as well as the timing of the biblical festivals, that they followed a similar agricultural calendar as we do today.

Most of us are isolated from that agricultural calendar. However, for the majority of human history, the ability of individuals or communities to survive the annual natural disaster known as winter depended on their ability to get seed in the ground, cultivate it and harvest between the time of the last frost in the spring and the first one in the fall. In the northern parts of our country, that's a rather narrow window of time.

Modern industrialized farming doesn't actually protect us from this threat; it merely isolates us from it. Should America's breadbasket suffer a freeze in the middle of July, there would be food shortages before the end of winter. How widespread those would be and how badly we would be affected would depend on how extensive the freeze is and how wealthy we are individually.

Throughout human history, mankind has lived preparing to survive the next disaster, even if that next disaster was nothing more than winter. It is only in modern times when we have become so highly dependent on our massive infrastructure that the idea of prepping has become novel.

Probably the clearest example of prepping we can find in the Bible is the story of Noah, found in Genesis

Chapters 6-8. We all know the story. God told Noah to build an ark (Genesis 6:14-16), a large boat, to save his family, as well as representatives of all animal species, from the coming flood — a flood of judgment for the sin of mankind.

This was not some random command from God. Rather, it was God's plan to save mankind and the animal kingdom from extinction. He made that clear to Noah, telling him:

> *I Myself am bringing floodwaters on the earth, to destroy from under heaven all flesh in which is the breath of life; everything that is on the earth shall die. But I will establish My covenant with you; and you shall go into the ark – you, your sons, your wife, and your sons' wives with you. And of every living thing of all flesh you shall bring two of every sort into the ark, to keep them alive with you; they shall be male and female (Genesis 6:17-19).*

So Noah built an ark. Theologians tell us that he spent 125 years working on that great project, all the while being mocked by his neighbors. They had never seen rain or a flood, so they were sure that Noah the prepper was nothing more than a fool with a loose screw. Yet, as we know, Noah was far from a fool. Rather, he was a God-fearing man who acted upon what God told him to do. He built the ark because God told him to and sure enough, when the ark was finished, God sent the flood.

In actuality, Noah did more than build the ark, for God directed him to provision it as well:

> *And you shall take for yourself of all food that is eaten, and you shall gather it to yourself; and it shall be food for you and for them (the animals) (Genesis 6:21).*

This verse is significant. It definitively shows the error of those who say we should not prepare but simply have faith in God to provide. Admittedly, Noah acted in faith; he continued to obey God for the 125 years it took him to build the ark. However, he also acted in faith to stock the ark with provisions, just as God told him.

Was Noah any less a man of faith because he provisioned the ark? By no means. If anything, he demonstrated faith (Hebrews 11). He heard from and trusted God. His faith was manifest in obedience.

It is important to note that these events did not happen as Hollywood depicts them. The clouds didn't part and a beam of light didn't descend on Noah. There was no deep, booming voice with lots of reverberation talking to him. No, God spoke to Noah, even as He did to the prophet Elijah.

> *And behold the Lord passed by, and a great and strong wind tore into the mountains and broke the rocks in pieces before the Lord, but the Lord was not in the wind; and after the wind an earthquake, but the Lord was not in*

*the earthquake; and after the earthquake a
fire, but the Lord was not in the fire; and aft
the fire a still small voice. So it was, when
Elijah heard it, that he wrapped his face in his
mantle and went out and stood in the entrance
of the cave. Suddenly a voice came to him, and
said, 'what are you doing here, Elijah?' (1 Kings
19:11-13).*

This is one of the clearest examples in Scripture of how God talks to His prophets. It is not always through obvious signs and wonders but through a still, small voice. Elijah, who was an experienced prophet at that time, recognized the voice for what it was and left the cave so God could speak to him.

Yet, that same voice of God convicted Noah of his need to obey and spend the next 125 years of his life managing the biggest building project attempted by any man to that day. His faith sustained him through those years in spite of the ridicule he received.

If Noah could hear from God that a disaster was about to come, why can't believers recognize the wisdom of God in Scripture? Perhaps the question we should be asking isn't whether or not we are prophets who hear from God as Noah did but if He has already spoken wisdom in His Word that we have missed or ignored. Scripture gives many warnings of pending disasters. If there is any chance that we have heard that voice giving us a warning, but we have not obeyed, then where is our faith?

In addition to the example of Noah, there are other biblical reasons for prepping. That is, the Bible makes it clear we have a responsibility to care for our families. Perhaps the best-known verse on this is found in Paul's first letter to Timothy:

> But if anyone does not provide for his own, and especially for those of his household, he has denied the faith and is worse than an unbeliever (1 Timothy 5:8).

Interestingly enough, this is the only place in Scripture where it says that a believer can be worse than an unbeliever. I'm sure that's not an accident. God takes our responsibility to care for our families as something serious. He doesn't accept excuses such as not having enough money or not knowing what we should do. Not knowing is never an acceptable excuse for failing to obey any of God's commands, why should His instruction to prepare be any different?

It is significant that this verse neither talks at all about God providing for our families nor does it say anything about us having faith in Him to do so. Rather, it seems to dump the responsibility directly in our laps, as if God, speaking through the apostle Paul, expects us to take care of them.

How can this possibly be denying the faith? Wouldn't it be a better example of faith for us to trust God to take care of us and our families, rather than doing so ourselves?

That depends a lot on the definition of faith that one uses. There are many today who preach faith as a tool for twisting God's arm and getting Him to do what they want. You know – things like giving them a new car or a bigger house – that sort of faith. But that sort of faith isn't taught in the Bible. It's especially not found in the "great hall of faith" talked about in Hebrews Chapter 11.

The great heroes of the faith who are mentioned in Hebrews Chapter 11 did not use their faith to twist God's arm and receive something from Him. Instead, they used their faith to obey God. That's what true faith is all about. Just look at these examples:

- *By faith, Abel offered God a more excellent sacrifice than Cain (Hebrews 11:4)*
- *By faith Noah, being divinely warned of things not yet seen, moved with godly fear, prepared an ark for the saving of his household (Hebrews 11:7)*
- *By faith, Abraham obeyed when he was called to go out to the place which he would receive an inheritance. And he went out, not knowing where he was going (Hebrews 11:8)*
- *By faith Abraham, when he was tested, offered up Isaac, and he who had received the*

promises offered up his only begotten son (Hebrews 11:17)
- *By faith Moses, when he was born, was hidden three months by his parents (Hebrews 11:23)*
- *By faith Moses, when he became of age, refused to be called the son of Pharaoh's daughter (Hebrews 11:24)*
- *By faith, the harlot Rahab did not perish with those who did not believe when she had received the spies with peace (Hebrews 11:31)*

If God is telling us to take care of our families and giving us the means to do so, is it not being faithful to obey Him? Isn't that true faith? According to the examples we find in the hall of faith it is. God makes it clear here, that the best sort of faith, is the one that inspires us to obey, regardless of the cost.

That might mean that we don't get to buy the new car or the big screen television we want. We may not get to have the bigger house we've dreamed of. In fact, we will have to give up many things we want and enjoy in the process of obeying God. Nevertheless, that too will be a demonstration that we are operating through faith, rather than satisfying the desires of our flesh.

From the examples shown in Hebrews Chapter 11, it is evident that there is a direct connection between the kind of faith God wants us to have and our obedience. That's the type of faith Paul was talking about in First Timothy. It's the type of faith that makes us do the right thing, not so much because God commands it of us but because we want to honor God with our lives.

Believers do not obey God to be saved, as there is no salvation in mere obedience. Salvation comes from accepting Jesus Christ as our Savior. We obey God because we are saved. Jesus made this clear to us:

> *If you love me, keep My commandments (John 14:15).*

Furthermore, Paul shows that we are not saved through obedience but by our faith:

> *We who are Jews by nature, and not sinners of the Gentiles, knowing that a man is not justified by the works of the law, but by faith in Jesus Christ (Galatians 2:15-16).*

What does this have to do with prepping? It is simple. When we prepare ourselves for disasters, we obey God by providing for and taking care of our families. God Himself established the family. Each member of the family unit is His child we have been entrusted with the responsibility to care for. As any father would, He appreciates our efforts on His behalf.

Chapter 4.

Stockpiling, the Beginning of All Prepping

While there is much more to being prepared than just stockpiling food, that seems to be the one place where everyone starts. Much like squirrels hiding acorns for the coming winter, we have an innate understanding of our need to stockpile food for an emergency. That's probably a good thing, as we humans don't seem to have too many other instincts that will help us survive a disaster.

Not only is stockpiling the beginning of all prepping; it is also an activity that continues throughout the rest of our lives. The truth is since none of us know what we will be facing in years to come, especially what potential disasters we might face, there's no way for us to say, "Now, I have enough." So, while we may start out with stockpiling, in a sense, we also end there as well.

Developing an effective stockpile also means developing a balanced stockpile. That is to say, you should have a well-proportioned mixture of necessities in your stockpile. I know a couple who started out prepping, and the first thing the woman did was buy two years' worth of toilet paper. I had to laugh. While toilet paper is important, it is not going to keep anyone alive.

If we accept the idea that we do not just need to stockpile food, what do we need to have in our stockpile? Here's a list just for starters.

- Purified water – You cannot trust any water sources in a survival situation as dysentery can kill
- Non-perishable food – Some will say to stockpile whatever your family eats, but this is incorrect. Few of us eat foods that will keep for more than a couple days or weeks
- Fuel – Both for cooking and for heating your home
- Fire starters – Matches, butane lighters, etc., as well as some sort of tinder or accelerant to make it easier to start the fire
- First-aid supplies – Chances are higher of getting injured during a crisis and it is harder to get medical care
- Over-the-counter medicines – For the same reason stated above
- Prescription medicines – If anyone in the family is taking them regularly
- Candles, oil lamps, and flashlights (along with oil & batteries) – Basic lighting supplies
- Pet food – For those who have pets

- Diapers & baby food – For those who have babies in the home. Baby wipes are useful for a lot of things
- Cash – It's always a good idea to have some cash on hand. If the power is out, your credit and debit cards won't do any good
- Personal hygiene supplies – This covers a broad range of items we all use every day
- Cleaning supplies – Cleanliness of the home is necessary to reduce the chances of having pests and the diseases they can bring
- Pest control – Disasters usually bring an increase in the insect and rodent population. If you want to keep them out of your home, you'll need to be ready. You'll also need insect repellent, as your home may be more open and exposed; you don't want to feed the mosquitoes
- Assorted plastic bags – You'll find a million uses for them
- Lime – Useful if you have to jury-rig a makeshift toilet. Lime will help keep the smell down and help avoid attracting insects

This list is by no means complete nor is it intended to be. I only wanted to kick-start your thinking by giving you an idea of the basic items you can stockpile. There are many complete lists on the internet that you can find. Of course, not all lists are equal. There are many different ideas about what you need depending on a variety of survival scenarios. You will need to combine what you can glean from various lists in order to have a complete list for yourself. Check the Resources page at the end of this book for a free download list I have put together you.

One of the biggest mistakes you can make is to try doing everything at once. That's just not possible, and most of us can't afford it anyway. A better approach is to start out small and try to get enough of everything to last your family a week. Once you have that, work on expanding it to two weeks, then a month. Keep adding additional supplies, month by month, until you feel you have enough to get you through any foreseeable crisis.

YOU NEED TO EQUIP YOUR HOME FOR SURVIVAL

In addition to stockpiling the supplies that you would use in a survival situation, you also need to stockpile the necessary equipment to use those supplies. Without going to extremes, here is a list of the basic equipment you need as part of your stockpile.

- Means of water purification – There's no way you can stockpile enough water for a long-term survival situation; therefore, you need some means of making water that you harvest safely to drink
- Means of cooking – If the power goes out, the gas might too. In that case, your stove isn't going to work. How are you going to cook your food?

- Manual kitchen tools – If the electricity is out, your appliances won't work. Do you have a manual eggbeater in your home?
- Means of heating your home – All home heating equipment require electricity to operate, which means they will not work if there is a power outage
- Alternate means of transportation – In case you can't get gasoline for your car
- Solar charger – For your cell phone and other batteries
- Arms and ammunition – You have to be able to defend yourself, just in case

As with the supplies above, these items are just a beginning to get you going. As you go farther along in your prepping, you will undoubtedly find many other things to add to this list.

Chapter 5.

Practical Skills to Help You Survive

When we're talking about prepping, we're not talking in terms of being prepared for only one sort of disaster as seen on "Doomsday Preppers." Rather, true preppers attempt to be prepared for any and all disasters they might encounter. Typically, some sort of risk analysis is done, albeit informally, to determine what sorts of disasters one might confront.

People who live in south Florida will probably never experience a winter blizzard. Likewise, the people living in Kansas aren't going to see a hurricane anytime soon. Each geographic location has its own specific types of natural disasters to be concerned about. However, as mentioned earlier, natural disasters aren't all we need to think of. There are various categories of disasters that should be included in our plans:

- Personal disasters – Something that just affects your family, such as the loss of a job, health problems or a house fire
- Natural disasters – Regional events that can disrupt power and the supply chain

- Man-made disasters – This varied category includes things like chemical spills, war, social unrest and a collapse of the economy
- TEOTWAWKI events – Anything that would keep us from returning to life as normal, such as a loss of the electrical power grid

Prepping is actually a mixed bag, combining stockpiling supplies, buying the right equipment and learning the right skills. Just stockpiling supplies (which is what most people start with) isn't enough. You might have a mountain of supplies and absolutely no idea what to do with them. Cooking can be a big problem when the electricity and gas are off. So it doesn't take long for most people who start prepping to realize they need to learn some skills as well.

While all three elements of prepping mentioned above are important, learning the right skills trumps the other two in importance. With the right skills, you can make up for a lack of equipment or supplies, but the converse isn't necessarily true. Eventually, your supplies will run out and if you don't have skills, you are sunk.

The skills needed for survival actually fall into four different categories:

- Bushcraft skills, such as how to start a fire and how to make a shelter out of naturally occurring materials. These are skills you would use in the wilderness, but an amazing amount of them are useful in urban survival as well

- Short-term urban survival skills such as water purification and how to do things without electricity
- Homesteading skills for long-term survival situations where you will need to raise your own food and preserve it yourself
- Trades-crafts such as blacksmithing or tanning for use in a TEOTWAWKI event. For example, an EMP, where we will have to rebuild society without the benefit of modern technology

As you can see, these four categories of skills form a progression based upon how long it takes for things to return to some semblance of normalcy after a disaster. If all you are ever confronted with is a natural disaster, then you will only need the first two categories of skills. However, as none of us has a crystal ball showing what the future holds for us, to be fully ready means to prepare for that potential TEOTWAWKI event. That involves learning homesteading skills, as well as, at least, some trades-craft that you can use in a post-disaster world.

Please note that in a post-disaster world, people's worth will be valued by these survival skills, especially in the case of a TEOTWAWKI event. If you have no skills then in a TEOTWAWKI you are useless to everyone. Lawyers and marketing specialists will be of little worth in such a case because their skills will not be needed. However, someone who can purify water, tan a hide or grow a vegetable garden will be highly valuable, not only to his/her family or survival team but to society in general.

This is why for committed preppers, training is not an action that has an end, even though it usually has a clearly defined start. The more time people spend as preppers, the more they learn, usually starting with the simpler skills and working their way up to understanding the more complex ones.

What are the basic skills preppers need to survive a disaster and the aftermath thereof?

- Fire starting – This means doing so without using charcoal starting fluid or some other chemical means
- Water purification – You may not be able to drink the city water
- Cooking over an open fire
- Keeping your home warm without the furnace – This is generally accomplished with a wood-burning stove, but other options such as kerosene are possible as well
- Food preservation techniques without electricity – Canning, smoking, dehydrating, etc.
- Where to find water – in the city and in the country

- Water harvesting techniques – Such as rainwater capture
- Cutting and splitting wood for a fire
- Building a shelter from natural materials
- Cross-country navigation using topographical maps and a compass
- Basic first-aid
- Self-defense techniques – Most likely shooting

Please note that this is pretty much a minimal list. It is meant only to show the kinds of skills that are needed to survive a short-term situation with you sheltering in place, as well as the absolute minimum amount of survival skills for wilderness survival.

THE SURVIVAL TEAM

You will be the best off, if you can become a part of a survival team. The amount of work and knowledge required for survival is so vast one person can't really do it all. A few hardy souls have survived alone such as the mountain men who trapped furs in America's past; however, they lived very primitive lifestyles while doing that.

The more comfort we want in our lives, the more work is required. Not only that, but a wider variety of skills are also essential. This is provided in modern society by the millions of people who supply the vast array of products and services we consume every day.

The idea of returning to a primitive lifestyle is not palatable to modern man. We are accustomed to our luxuries. And while we may not have those luxuries in the wake of a disaster, we will try to recreate as many of them as we can, as quickly as we can. I am not talking about the internet and television here, as those probably won't come back in any haste. I am referring to being able to buy items like off-the-shelf groceries and clothes. I just don't see people reverting to wearing buckskins.

Even the absolute minimum for survival requires a significant amount of work. I am talking about the basic needs of shelter, heat, water, food, limited medical supplies, and self-defense. While one person can learn enough to take care of that for him/herself, one person working alone can't provide that for an entire family. Moreover, the longer time goes on, the less that person will be able to provide any of it single-handedly.

The key, therefore, is to form a community of like-minded people who will make plans on gathering together to survive in the wake of a disaster. This group could be your extended family or your neighborhood. However, it will most likely end up consisting of a group of friends and co-workers you encounter who have accepted the need to prepare just as you have.

At a minimum, this group will need the following skills:

- Leadership – Someone has to be the leader

- Bushcraft or survival skills – At least one person who is an expert
- Infantry or defense – Someone to coordinate your team's defenses
- Medical – A team medic to take care of injuries and minor sicknesses
- General repairs – You're going to end up breaking things and need a general handyman who can fix anything
- Gardening – To grow food
- Animal husbandry – Also to grow food
- Food preservation – To keep that food edible through the winter

For a more serious or longer-term survival situation such as a TEOTWAWKI event, you may want to consider adding the following skills to your team:

- Communications – Probably via Ham radio
- Midwifery – Could be the team medic or a woman in the team
- Hunting – For harvesting food from nature
- Fishing – Ditto
- Woodworking – To make furniture, repair homes and make wood tools
- Blacksmithing – To make and repair metal tools
- Counselor – A minister or someone who has training as a counselor for those struggling to adapt to the situation

- Tanning/leatherworking – To turn hides into leather for shoes and harnesses
- Sewing/weaving – To make clothing
- Teacher – To teach the next generation of children

Obviously, a community will need even more skills than this in the event of a disaster. All we're talking about are the skills for a survival team. While that is a community of sorts, it is hoped that over time, survival teams will unite to form the nucleus of rebuilding communities.

Please note that each skill doesn't necessarily denote one person. Some skills listed above will only be needed occasionally. Others (like gardening) will require everyone pitching in and working. Individuals can learn multiple skills, reducing the overall headcount. At the same time, people whose skills are not needed all the time should be expected to pitch in and help with community work like growing food.

INTRODUCING PREPPERNET.COM

The hard part of finding a survival team or group is knowing where to find like-minded people who are concerned about being prepared for disasters and taking responsibility for their own readiness. You can't just advertise in the newspaper or on Craig's List and expect to find a group. Most preppers try to keep what they are doing quiet, practicing what is known as OPSEC (operational security) a military term that applies directly to us.

Maintaining OPSEC is important because when things turn bad, all those people out there who are not prepared aren't going to know what to do. Sadly, over 98% of our population actually thinks that FEMA will bail them out and take care of them. That's not true, especially in any nationwide cataclysmic event.

It is said that desperate people do desperate things. Hence, when millions of people out there realize the government does not have the capacity to provide them with truckloads of free food and other necessities, they're going to become desperate, especially those with hungry kids. When that happens, they're going to be looking for help wherever they can find it.

The first wave of violence will be looting the stores and will happen within 72 hours of the disaster as people try to get what they need from stores. These stores will be caught in the chaos as they can no longer accept credit and debit cards to facilitate purchases. Those who have cash will try to buy what they need legally. However, those who don't will quickly turn into a looting mob, taking what they need and knocking down anyone who gets in their way.

Inevitably, the supplies they get from looting the stores will only last them a few days. The average grocery store stocks only three days worth of inventory and when that runs out, there won't be any resupply. Consequently, people will start looking around to see who has what they need. Naturally, their eyes will fall on those who are preppers — if they know who we are.

That's why OPSEC is so important. You may be able to turn people away the first time when they come knocking on your door looking for food. However, it will be harder to do that when they gang together and show up with guns in their hands. Hopefully, OPSEC will keep that from happening.

I believe God has called me to prepare the saints for the tough times that are coming. We are to be warriors for Christ in these last days. That is why for the last 17 years, I have been training, studying, and getting myself ready for this calling. I am now a survival instructor, NRA instructor, general license HAM operator, Krav Maga apprentice instructor, speaker, educator, radio/podcast host, and author. For years, I was so private about my training that even my closest friends were unaware of my survival and preparedness activities.

Out of my calling, I founded PrepperNet. Actually, PrepperNet was started a number of years ago, in 2014, when I started the Carolina Preppers Network (CPN). The organization quickly grew to 8,700 members with chapters in 21 different cities. But things didn't stop there. It didn't take long for our vision to unite and support preppers to grow beyond the Carolinas. Like-minded people everywhere were getting prepared and needed help in organizing what we call "city teams." Many of these people lived outside the Carolinas, making our name a bit obsolete, so we changed it to the simpler "PrepperNet." Our website can be found at www.PrepperNet.com.

While all this expansion was going on, we developed an extensive training program for our city leaders. Our comprehensive city leader training program provides everything needed to establish and develop an extensive group. This includes:

- A city meetup plan
- Instructions on how to establish a communications team
- Marketing plan
- Support forums
- City Zello nets and how to manage them
- Presentation downloads
- Monthly conference calls
- Online city leader directory
- Support via e-mail, phone, and text from our expert panel

PrepperNet is an organization of like-minded individuals who believe in personal responsibility, individual freedoms, and seriously preparing for disasters of all types. As such, PrepperNet is aimed at individuals who have an interest in gaining knowledge, acquiring new skills and most importantly, networking with other like-minded individuals who have a preparedness mindset.

Here at PrepperNet, we have set the following goals:

- Provide a venue for like-minded individuals interested in disaster preparedness to meet in their local area. While 90% networking – 10% training/fun, this provides members the opportunity to interact and assist in creating Mutual Assistance Groups (MAGS) and communities.
- Connect Preppers across the United States with our Opt-in/Opt-out real-time directory while providing OPSEC for all.
- Partnering with AmRRON, PrepperNet is in the process of creating a nationwide emergency communications plan.
- Provide an expert panel of industry leaders to help train, motivate, and unite preppers.
- Unite preppers at a local level. This includes providing trained group leaders with the tools needed to run successful groups.
- PrepperNet has partnered with the Americans Networking to Survive – A.N.T.S is a survival network of individual preppers working together to provide other members with basic supplies during disasters.
- Create a nationwide network of local PrepperNet groups and regional and national level training events.

Our PrepperNet Expert Panel consists of industry experts such as John Jacob Schmidt, Scott Hunt, Charley Hogwood, Dr. Bones & Nurse Amy, Glen Tate, Shelby Gallagher, Samuel J Culper, Survivor Jane, Rick Austin, Ryan Mitchell, Franklin Horton, and Brian Duff with more to be added soon.

PrepperNet has two different membership levels:

- PrepperNet Basic – This is a FREE membership program that allows preppers to join PrepperNet and participate in our Facebook groups, search and join their local PrepperNet Meetup groups and take advantage of the PrepperNet discount-buying program.
- PrepperNet Premium Level – Our paid membership program. Premium members get the PrepperNet Alert App, Access to our Zello Channels, free online subscription to PREPARE Magazine, Opt-in/Opt-out Membership map, and the AmRRON/PrepperNet Nation-wide communications plan. Furthermore, the Premium members get full access to our forums, monthly webinars, training, recommendations, and access to the PrepperNet expert panel.

Danger is ever present; however, our country has never faced the potential for disaster as we do today. Never before in the history of our nation was it as necessary as it is today for like-minded individuals to unite across America and take responsibility for their own disaster preparedness.

If you want more information about PrepperNet, please check out our website at www.PrepperNet.com or email me personally at fg@preppernet.com.

Chapter 6.

Faith, Our Most Important Prep

The prepping community has many different types of people in it. While it started out amongst political conservatives, more and more people on the left side of the political spectrum are joining our ranks. One hotbed of this is in Silicon Valley, where the high-tech newly-rich are buying or building survival retreats as far away as New Zealand. But for our purposes, preppers can be broken down a different way: between those who believe in Jesus Christ and those who don't. This is an important distinction because it can greatly affect our attitude and reasoning as we prepare.

Any military survival manual you pick up (and there are a lot of them) always starts out with a chapter about mental attitude. That's because a positive mental attitude is one of the most important parts of surviving anything. They're even finding out that a positive mental attitude increases the chances of a cancer patient's survival.

People who have positive mental attitudes will do whatever they need to with all their hearts and strength to survive. On the other hand, those who have negative mental attitudes will have trouble seeing the advantage of trying hard and are just as likely to give up.

So what does that have to do with our faith? Those with a strong faith in Jesus Christ are much more likely to have positive mental attitudes than those who don't. Christianity and the Bible in general, provide a very positive message, even though the world doesn't see it that way. All they see is that the Ten Commandments tells them not to do things they want to do. They project that onto the rest of the Bible saying it is all a list of things they can't do.

But the Bible and the gospel message are far from that. It is the message of hope through salvation. That's a very positive message in which God Himself has paid the price for us, saving us from our sinful nature, so we can be in a relationship with Him. It's not so much about what we do, as it is about what He has already done for us.

Of course, we have a part to play in salvation just as we do in anything else God does for us. In the case of salvation, we have to admit we are sinners and accept as fact that Jesus died for our sins and on the third day, He rose from the dead. That's actually a very small price to pay for what we get in return. However, there is something most people miss: the full meaning of the word "salvation." Salvation doesn't just apply to the act of being saved spiritually from our sins. It also refers to us being saved physically from anything we need saving from. In other words, Jesus Christ and His Father, God, didn't just save us from our sins. The work of the cross saves us from any and everything we need saving from, spiritually or physically. We can apply that to sickness, poverty, oppression, abuse, and even a disaster, which is threatening our very survival.

Some might take what I just said as a contradiction to what I said earlier about us having to do our part in preparing for a disaster; however, drawing such a conclusion is wrong. If we are going to be saved from our sins, we have to do our part (i.e., believing the gospel), likewise, if we are going to be saved from a deadly situation (i.e., a disaster).

Here's the thing that we have going for us though. Those of us who are believers in Christ don't have to depend simply on what we do; we can also depend on God to take what we've done and fill in where we've missed. Said differently, we can count on His help to make up for our lack.

This is actually included in God's grace. Most Christians define the word "grace" as "receiving what we don't deserve," specifically referring to receiving blessings that we don't deserve. That is an acceptable definition. However, grace also includes a much deeper aspect. God made that clear to the apostle Paul when he was struggling with problems in his own life.

> *And lest I should be exalted above measure by*
> *the abundance of the revelations, a thorn in the*
> *flesh was given to me, a messenger of Satan to*
> *buffet me, lest I be exalted above measure.*
> *Concerning this thing I pleaded with the Lord*
> *three times that it might depart from me. And*
> *He said to me, "My grace is sufficient for you,*
> *for My strength is made perfect in weakness"*
> *(2 Corinthians 12:7-9).*

What was God actually teaching Paul here? I can't see where He said, "I gave you my grace, so you don't have to put up with that." Nor can I see where He said, "I gave you my grace, so that thorn in the flesh you're complaining about doesn't exist." Rather, I see Him saying, "I know you are too weak to handle this on your own but instead of taking it from you, I'll give you my grace. That will get you through the problem, but it won't help you to avoid it."

You see, God doesn't necessarily take away our problems, as much as we might like Him to. Rather, He uses those problems to help us grow. What else could Romans 8:28-29 possibly mean?

> *And we know that all things work together for*
> *good to those who love God, to those who are*
> *the called according to His purpose. For whom*
> *He foreknew, He also predestined to be*
> *conformed to the image of His Son, that He*
> *might be the firstborn among many brethren.*
> *(Romans 8:28-29)*

So God allows problems to come into our lives. That's scriptural. But God doesn't expect us to deal with those problems on our own. Yes, He expects us to do our part but then, once we've done that, He expects us to depend on Him regardless of the outcome. He expects us to use the grace that He has freely given us to make it through the problem.

You've Got to Have Faith in Order to Use It

Some believers never take their faith beyond the initial act of trusting in God for salvation. There are many cases in the gospels where Jesus upbraided people for not having enough faith, and He wasn't talking about not having enough faith to get saved. He was talking about not having faith for healing, for provision and to survive trials and difficulties of all kinds.

Remember when Jesus and His disciples were crossing the Sea of Galilee and a storm came (Mark 4:35-40)? Jesus was asleep in the back of the boat until His disciples woke Him deeply concerned they would perish in the storm. That sounds like a survival situation. What was Jesus' response to them?

> *Why are you so fearful? How is it that you have no faith? (Mark 4:40).*

In verse 35, Jesus had told them, "*Let us cross over to the other side.*" This is the Son of God speaking. He gave an instruction; hence, it was possible to do. There was no other option. Yet, the disciples were petrified.

Jesus rebuked them. Why?

Had they truly had faith, they would have understood that there was enough power in Jesus' words to get them to the other side, regardless of what the wind and the waves did. Isn't that what faith is, believing what God says about something? Faith is not, "God said it; I believe it; that settles is." Rather, it is, "God said it; that settles it; I'd better believe it."

One of the many things that God has promised us is His presence and protection. So, "God said it; that settles it; I'd better believe it." But just how do I do that?

To start with, the Bible tells us *"God has dealt to each one a measure of faith"* (Romans 12:3). So we all have some faith, however much a measure is.

I can tell you from my personal experience, as well as the experience of many others, that faith which is used, grows. What do I mean by "faith that is used?" I mean praying for things and trusting God to bring them to pass. Start small, like praying for your children's healing when they are sick. As your faith grows, you can then use it to pray for bigger things.

Why is this important? Because some day, you are going to need a lot of faith in God. You're going to need to know that He will come through for you. And if you have never used your faith, you are not going to be ready. Instead, you are going to be like those disciples in the boat saying, *"Don't you care that we are perishing?"*

Applying Your Faith to a Survival Scenario

If you exercise your faith as I just described, and you have prepared as well, you will be better equipped spiritually and physically to face any survival situation than those whose faith has not been used. When that disaster strikes, not only will you have food, water, and other critical supplies, you will also know how to depend on God.

As part of this, I highly recommend making yourself a list of written scripture verses that you can use in prayer, which talk about God's protection and provision for you. Laminate it, so it can't get damaged by the rain and keep it with whatever other information you gather for disaster preparedness. We are to pray in agreement with God's Word. The best possible way of doing that is to know what His Word says about a given situation.

Now, we have three different things we can add together to survive a disaster; they are:

- Your preparations
- Your faith
- God's grace

These three things fit together like the three cords of a rope; each of them supporting the other and creating a capability that is stronger than the sum of their parts. Your preparations provide the basic needs of your family, while you pray and trust God. The faith that you've been building will allow you to pray, trusting in God's grace to make up for your shortcomings. And finally, the grace of God will meet your needs also filling in where you fall short.

Being specific in your prayers will be important. "Shotgun prayers" where people just say something like, "God, we're trusting you to take care of us" aren't as effective as praying for specific, identifiable needs. So you'll need to know what those needs are.

That means you must be as well-informed about your situation as you can be. To do that, you will need to be plugged into good sources of information where you can find out what is going on. Knowing that another storm is coming, for example, will tell you that you need to be praying for the storm to pass you by or for the storm not to drop so much water that it increases flooding.

In addition, you will need to pray for God to take care of problems specific to your family and your family's situation. This can include a long list of things such as:

- Health issues that specific family members have
- Protection from attacks by people who are not prepared
- Providing for things that you might not have stockpiled adequately

- Protection from the weather
- Protection for your home, vehicles, and other tools to prevent damage.

Obviously, you will need to add to that list based upon your own needs. The list I provided is to simply give you an idea of what types of things to think of. Make a list of the things you will need God's help with and pray about those things every day.

God will be with you in the situation, and He will protect you as long as you pray in faith believing that He will. That does not mean nothing bad will befall you. God isn't going to encapsulate you in a bubble, while everyone around you is suffering. However, His grace will see you through the situation.

Chapter 7.

One Last Thing You Need

As we have said, having faith is an important part of surviving any potential disaster. Therefore, I have to ask, do you have faith? I don't mean some general, wishy-washy, unspecified faith; I'm talking about faith in Jesus Christ as your personal Lord and Savior.

"What does that have to do with surviving?" you might ask. Everything. The truth of the matter is that there is only so much you and I can do. There are forces in nature that are much stronger than we are, not to mention some of the massive forces that mankind can produce. But no matter how big any of them are, they cannot be compared to God, for He not only created this world but sustains it.

The reality of the situation is that while God expects us to do our part, He doesn't abandon us to do it alone. I know many people don't believe that, but I have experienced His help enough in my life to be absolutely sure of it. When the next crisis comes along, I want to be on God's side.

Does that mean God will protect me from all suffering? By no means. The Bible gives plenty of examples of believers who suffered, and there are also many who are recorded in church history. But the one outstanding thing about those examples is that they didn't go through hardship alone. God, through Jesus Christ, was with them.

We need not look any further than the Middle Ages to find some of the most outstanding examples of God being with believers in the midst of their trials. When I read about men like John Hus who was burned at the stake, I see the hand of God moving in his life. He was so unaffected by the fiery torment that he sang songs of glory to God right up to the moment he died without any indication he was in pain,

Does having God with you guarantee a safe passage? Sadly, I can't say that it does. That same example of John Hus shows me there is no such surety. But it does guarantee us that when we have done all that we can, and we breathe our last breath, we will find ourselves in the presence of an all-loving God where there is no suffering or pain. We will be in a place where we will never have to concern ourselves about another disaster striking because there won't be any.

I'm talking, of course, about heaven, the final destination of every believer in Jesus Christ. That's God's promise to us. Those of us who have accepted Jesus Christ as our personal Lord and Savior will spend eternity there with Him.

> *We are confident, yes, well pleased rather to be absent from the body and to be present with the Lord (2 Corinthians 5:8).*

In the mean time, as long as we are here on this earth, we have the promise that He is with us and will always be.

> *He Himself has said, 'I will never leave you nor forsake you' (Hebrews 13:5).*

This is possibly even better expressed through a well-known piece of poetry known by Christians as "Footprints in the Sand."

> *One night I had a dream.*
> *As I was walking along the beach with my Lord.*
> *Across the dark sky flashed scenes from my life.*
> *For each scene, I noticed two sets of footprints in the sand,*
> *One belonging to me and one to my Lord.*
> *After the last scene of my life flashed before me,*
> *I looked back at the footprints in the sand.*
> *I noticed that at many times along the path of my life,*
> *especially at the very lowest and saddest times,*
> *there was only one set of footprints.*
> *This really troubled me, so I asked the Lord about it.*
> *"Lord, you said once I decided to follow you,*
> *You'd walk with me all the way.*

But I noticed that during the saddest and most
troublesome times of my life,
there was only one set of footprints.
I don't understand why, when I needed You the
most, You would leave me."
He whispered, "My precious child, I love you
and would never leave you
Never, ever, during your trials and testings.
When you saw only one set of footprints,
it was then that I carried you.

- Anonymous

That's the promise to those of us who have accepted Jesus Christ as our Lord and Savior. When disasters come and times get bad, it is then He will carry us. While everyone else is trying to survive the disaster on their own, we will have the help they don't. It won't be visible; it may not be obvious, but it will be there nevertheless. And by faith, His help will see us through.

ARE YOU SAVED?

This brings us back to the question I started this chapter off with: do you have faith? Specifically, do you have faith in Jesus Christ as your Lord and Savior? You can. God is offering salvation to you as a free gift, even now as you read these words.

Like any gift, salvation has to be received. If someone were to offer you the keys and title to a brand new car the vehicle would be no good to you until you receive them. That title might have your name on it, but you would still have to accept the gift. So it is with salvation.

Jesus came to earth for the express purpose of calling the lost and offering them salvation. All of us are lost in our sins until we receive the salvation that He offers us. It's actually quite easy.

First, we must understand and accept the fact that we have sinned. In other words, we've done wrong things in life, rather than the right things. We all do because none of us is perfect. But God knows we cannot perfect ourselves. Hence, God sent His Son Jesus to do that for us.

> *For all have sinned and come short of the glory of God (Romans 3:23).*

It doesn't matter how many "good things" we've done; they are not enough. One sin is enough to ensure we are on the road to eternal separation from God. What the Bible calls hell. But that's not God's desire for us. He doesn't send anyone to hell; we're going there on our own volition by continuing to reject God's offer of salvation. Our sin or disobedience to Him separates us from Him for all eternity.

> *For the wages of sin is death, but the gift of God is eternal life through Jesus Christ His Son (Romans 6:23).*

God knows that none of us is perfect. That's why Jesus

died on the cross. He became the perfect offering for our sins because He has no sin. Therefore, He was able to pay the penalty of death for each and every one of us.

> *But God commanded His love toward us, in that, while we were yet sinners, Christ died for us (Romans 5:8).*

So the work is done; all we have to do is accept it. That means accepting the fact that we are sinners and Jesus died for our sins. Jesus, the only begotten Son of God, died personally for each and every one of us. He paid that price. All we have to do is accept the free gift.

> *For whoever shall call upon the name of the Lord shall be saved (Romans 10:13).*

But the story doesn't end at the cross. Jesus died and was buried, but He rose from the dead. We celebrate this every year at Easter. His death paid the price for our sins, but His resurrection has given us new life. It has guaranteed that our bodies will also rise from physical death, and we will be with Him in eternity.

> *That is thou shall confess with thy mouth the Lord Jesus, and shell believe in your heart that God raised Him from the dead, you shall be saved (Romans 10:9).*

If you've never accepted Jesus Christ as your personal Lord and Savior, as I just described above, why not do so now? All it takes is one short prayer. Use the prayer below as a pattern for yours. It is not the words that save you but the attitude of your heart. Your prayer must be sincere; it must come from your heart.

> *Dear God, I realize and confess that I have fallen short of Your best for my life; I am a sinner. I thank You for making provision for me, in that Jesus Christ, Your Son died on the cross, taking upon Himself the penalty for my sins. That's something I could never do for myself. I recognize how awesome that work was for me, as well as acknowledging that He didn't stay in that grave but rose from dead by Your mighty power on the third day. I accept Your free gift of Salvation and thank You for it. I thank You for accepting me as Your child and that I will now be able to spend eternity with You.*

If you just prayed that prayer for the first time, I would like to be the first to welcome you into God's family. You are now an entirely new person: a child of God. Through the next months and years, you will see God working in your life, teaching you new things and helping you to grow and mature in this new life.

It is our great pleasure to be here for you along that journey, encouraging you, praying for you, and helping you to grow.

Please, contact us right away to let us know about the

decision you have made. We want to rejoice with you and start praying for you immediately.

Please visit our website at https://thecaseforchristianpreparedness.com/onelastthing and let us know your response!

Thank you and God bless you on your new journey.

ABOUT THE AUTHOR

Forrest Garvin is a former US Air Force NCO who served with the 317 MAC and JSOC SOLLII out of Pope Air Force Base. After leaving the military, Garvin worked in the technology field for the Strategic Technology Group for NationsBank/Bank of America and then went on to create several technology startups. Garvin is a survival instructor, NRA instructor, general license HAM operator, Krav Maga apprentice instructor, speaker, educator, radio/podcast host, and author. Garvin has been a prepper since Y2K. Garvin also owns the Carolina Survival & Preparedness Academy in Charlotte, NC. His survival academy offers courses in self-defense, homesteading, firearms, family preparedness and survival skills. In addition, he consults with preppers and survival groups around the USA. Garvin was the founder of the Carolina Preppers Network, which now is PrepperNet. PrepperNet has over 17,500 members nationwide.

forrest@thecaseforchristianpreparedness.com

RESOURCES

The Case For Christian Preparedness Website:
http://thecaseforchristianpreparedness.com

Authors Website:
http://forrestgarvin.com

Preppers Consulting:
https://preppersconsulting.com

Link to online resources:
https://thecaseforchristianpreparedness.com/resources

Want to know more about the Christian Faith?
Billy Graham Evangelistic Association:
https://peacewithgod.net

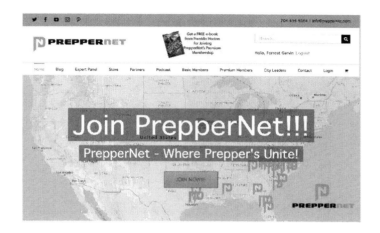

PrepperNet is the place to meet, network & find other preppers.

If you are not in a group... You will die.

For more resources and tools join us at PrepperNet
Website: https://preppernet.com

Signup for our Newsletter
Get a Free Bug Out Bag Check List

The Prepping Academy Radio Show!

Prepping Academy Radio Show is a live broadcast where we discuss all things prepping, survival and self-reliance. Our Goal at The Prepping Academy Radio Show is to expand your thinking & motivate you to take action – because it's time that we get prepared.

Host: Tenderfoot & Forrest

Website: https://preppingacademy.com

God Bless!

Made in United States
Troutdale, OR
02/25/2024

17976385R00042